For Grandmother,
with love and gratitude.

Published by:
Beyond Words Publishing, Inc.
13950 N.W. Pumpkin Ridge Road
Hillsboro, OR 97123
Phone: 503-647-5109
Toll Free: 1-800-284-9673
FAX: 503-647-5114

Printed in Canada
Distributed to the book trade by Publishers Group West

ISBN: 0-941831-29-9 Soft Cover
ISBN: 0-941831-21-3 Hard Cover

Library of Congress Catalog Number: 89:062534

Other Titles by Paul Owen Lewis:
The Starlight Bride
Davy's Dream
Ever Wondered?
Grasper

For information about a school lecture and slide show of
Paul Lewis' books, please contact Beyond Words Publishing.

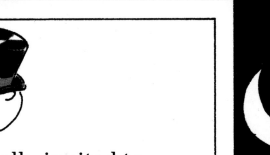

You are cordially invited to

P. BEAR'S

NEW YEAR'S PARTY!

(Formal dress required.)

A Counting book by

PAUL OWEN LEWIS

Mr. P.Bear decided to have sent invitations to his

a New Year's Party, and
best dressed friends.

At one o'clock, New

Year's Eve, a whale arrived...

at two o'clock, a

couple of horses...

at three o'clock, a

few dairy cows...

at four o'clock, a

herd of zebras...

at five o'clock, a

bunch of panda bears...

at six o'clock, a

half-dozen mountain goats...

at seven o'clock,

several snow leopards...

at eight o'clock, a

pack of dalmatian dogs...

at nine o'clock, lots

of skunks...

at ten o'clock, a

flock of geese....

at eleven o'clock, a

crowd of cats...

and, just before twelve

midnight, a dozen penguins!

How many guests came to the party?